Rory's Dance

Written by Jenny Feely

Illustrated by Meredith Thomas

Flying Start
to Literacy®

T0363487

Contents

Chapter 1:
Just a little different

Rory was a lion. She looked just like all the other lions in her pride.

The pride was Rory's family. It wasn't just her mother and father; it was all the lions and cubs that lived together.

But there was something different about Rory.

When the other cubs were hungry,
they growled to tell their mother.
But when Rory was hungry,
she sang a little song.

"Lions do not sing," her mother said.
"When you want milk, you must growl."

But Rory could not growl.
She was different.

Chapter 2:
A song and a dance

Rory wanted to be like the other lions in her pride. So one day when her pride went hunting, Rory went too.

As the lions moved slowly through the grass, Rory did too. And when the lions moved closer to the zebras, Rory did too.

But then Rory heard the grass go
Shhh! Shhh! Shhh!

And she heard the zebras' feet go
Tap! Tap! Tap!

And she heard the birds sing
Cheep! Cheep! Cheep!

Rory's tail began to move.

Then her body began to move.

She just had to dance.

And then she started to sing.

The zebras looked up and saw Rory dancing. And then they saw the lions getting closer and closer. The zebras quickly ran away.

"Rory," said her mother. "You cannot sing and dance when we are hunting!"

"If you do not stop singing and dancing," said her father,
"you will have to stay home when we go hunting."

"I can't stop," said Rory.
"I have to sing and dance."

Chapter 3:
All by herself

The next day, when the pride went
hunting, Rory had to stay at home.
She was all by herself.
She danced all by herself
and she sang all by herself.

Rory wanted to be with her mother.
She wanted to be with her father.
She wanted to hunt with the pride again.

"I know," said Rory. "I will watch the
pride every day and I will learn how
to be like the other lions."

The next time the pride went hunting, Rory sat on top of a hill. She watched the lions as they moved closer and closer to the zebras.

Suddenly, Rory saw something moving in the long, dry grass.

It was a lion hunter! The lion hunter's clothes were the same colour as the grass. The lions in the pride did not know that the lion hunter was there.

Rory had to do something.

Rory jumped up and roared her loudest
roar, but all that came out was
a squeak.

The hunter moved closer and closer
to the pride. Soon it would be too late.

Chapter 4:
Rory to the rescue

Then Rory had an idea.

She began to move her tail.
She began to move her body.

She started to sing
and she started to dance.

It was the loudest and craziest song
and dance that Rory had ever done.

The zebras looked up.
The lions looked up.
And the lion hunter looked up.

The zebras saw the lions.

The lions saw the hunter.

The hunter saw Rory.

And they all ran away!

And that was how Rory saved the pride.

Chapter 5:
Rory's pride

From that day on, when the lions go hunting out on the grasslands, things are a little different.

The lions creep through the tall, dry grass. They don't make a sound.

Rory sits on top of a hill and watches the lions hunt. And she is ready to sing and dance whenever she is needed.

A note from the author

I've always liked people who are true to themselves – people who know what they want from life and who they want to be, people who are just a bit different from everyone else.

So when Rory the singing and dancing lion popped into my head, I just had to tell her story. It's not easy being different from other people and it certainly wasn't for Rory, but I believe that everyone has a place if we give them time and space to find it. And look what happened to Rory and her pride when she followed her heart and was truly herself.